HOW TO GROW
BULB VEGETABLES

HOW TO GROW
BULB VEGETABLES

A PRACTICAL GARDENING GUIDE TO GROWING ONIONS, GARLIC, SHALLOTS, LEEKS, CHIVES AND FENNEL, WITH STEP-BY-STEP TECHNIQUES AND 165 PHOTOGRAPHS

RICHARD BIRD

southwater

This edition is published by Southwater, an
imprint of Anness Publishing Ltd, Hermes House,
88–89 Blackfriars Road, London SE1 8HA;
tel. 020 7401 2077; fax 020 7633 9499

www.southwaterbooks.com
www.annesspublishing.com

If you like the images in this book and would
like to investigate using them for publishing,
promotions or advertising, then please visit
our website www.practicalpictures.com for
more information.

UK distributor: Book Trade Services;
tel. 0116 2759086; fax 0116 2759090;
uksales@booktradeservices.com;
exportsales@booktradeservices.com
North American distributor: National Book
Network; tel. 301 459 3366; fax 301 429 5746;
www.nbnbooks.com
Australian distributor: Pan Macmillan Australia;
tel. 1300 135 113; fax 1300 135 103;
customer.service@macmillan.com.au
New Zealand distributor: David Bateman Ltd;
tel. (09) 415 7664; fax (09) 415 8892

Publisher: Joanna Lorenz
Managing Editor: Judith Simons
Project Editor: Felicity Forster
Photographers: Jonathan Buckley, Patrick
     McLeavey and William Lingwood
Front Cover Photographer: Gus Filgate
Illustrator: Liz Pepperell
Designer: Michael Morey
Editorial Reader: Penelope Goodare
Production Controller: Steve Lang

ETHICAL TRADING POLICY
Because of our ongoing ecological investment
programme, you, as our customer, can have the
pleasure and reassurance of knowing that a tree
is being cultivated on your behalf to naturally
replace the materials used to make the book you
are holding. For further information about this
scheme, go to www.annesspublishing.com/trees

Previously published as *Growing Bulb Vegetables*

PUBLISHER'S NOTE
Although the advice and information in this
book are believed to be accurate and true at the
time of going to press, neither the authors nor
the publisher can accept any legal responsibility
or liability for any errors or omissions that may
have been made nor for any inaccuracies nor for
any loss, harm or injury that comes about from
following instructions or advice in this book.

Contents

Introduction

All gardeners who are interested in what they eat would do well to consider the possibility of growing their own vegetables. Mounting concerns about the residues of fungicides, pesticides, artificial fertilizers and other chemicals in and on our foods have been intensified by the use of genetically modified crops and the realization that it is almost impossible to know exactly what it is that we are putting in our own mouths and, perhaps more importantly, in the mouths of our children, as well as the rest of our family.

Growing vegetables in our own gardens, on even a small scale, is the perfect way to ensure you have the healthiest possible produce. When you eat vegetables that you have grown yourself from seed or from sets bought from a reputable supplier you know that they are free from all taint of chemical. Even if you choose not to grow organically, you can use the minimum of artificial pesticides and fertilizers and time their applications so that you do not eat anything that has been recently sprayed.

GROWING YOUR OWN

The pre-packaged produce we buy in supermarkets may look tempting, but the flavour is often disappointing. Cultivars for home-grown vegetables are selected for flavour instead of uniformity and shelf-life, and when we have become used to insipid commercial produce, the taste can be a revelation – especially when the vegetables are freshly picked, rather than transported over long distances.

People are often deterred from growing vegetables, partly because it is so easy to buy a range of unusual crops in the supermarket and partly because vegetables have a reputation for requiring a lot of effort. Most gardeners, however, are

BELOW All types of onion are easy to grow and can be used in a wide range of dishes all year round.

ABOVE Chives have a more subtle flavour than onions. The leaves and flowerheads, but not the flower stalks, are edible.

perfectly happy to sow seeds of half-hardy annuals or to cut back and divide perennials, and may spend hours tending their lawn – cutting it, raking it, aerating it, fertilizing it and weeding it. Growing vegetables involves many of the same techniques, but rather than putting the dead plants on the compost heap at the end of the year, the vegetables are destined for the kitchen and dining table.

If you have a small area of the garden to devote to vegetables, members of the *Allium* genus are likely to be among the crops you will try. Not only are they easy to grow, but they are some of the most often used vegetables in the kitchen. Alliums range from the familiar large bulbs of the yellow- and brown-skinned onions to the small, round bulbs, no more than 2.5cm/1in across, of pickling onions. A row of onions or leeks takes up little space, and a clump of chives can be grown in a container by the back door so that you can snip off a few leaves whenever you need them. Florence fennel has the same attractive, feathery fronds as the related herb, and a few plants can be grown in a flower bed or border to provide you with the bulbs.

HARVESTING

All vegetables taste better when they are freshly harvested just before being used, which is one of the great advantages of home-grown vegetables. There are several types of onion, which can be sown from late winter to late summer, giving a year-round supply. Allow the leaves of the ripening bulbs to die back naturally, then carefully lift the onions with a fork, taking care that you do not pierce the bulbs.

Garlic and shallots are harvested when the leaves begin to turn brown. Leeks are sufficiently hardy to be left in the ground and lifted as required in autumn and winter. Florence fennel is harvested when the bulbs are plump and round.

COOKING

The shorter the period between harvesting and cooking, the better the flavour and the greater the nutritional content of all vegetables. Chives and spring onions are, of course, usually eaten raw in salads or as garnishes for cooked dishes. There can be few soups and casseroles that do not include onions, garlic or milder shallots, and these vegetables can also be used raw in salads. Leeks are also delicious in soups, and Florence fennel is usually boiled and served as a traditional accompaniment to fish or chicken, although the bulbs can also be grated and used raw in salads or as a garnish.

BELOW Red onions, roasted and served with melted cheese and herbs, make a simple yet delicious first course.

types of
bulb
vegetables

Most bulb vegetables are types of onion
and are members of the Alliaceae family.
They range from the large, uniform globes
of onions themselves to the multiple bulbs
of shallots. Garlic, too, with papery skins
enclosing the individual cloves, is a type
of onion, as are leeks, with their slim,
upright stems. The leaf bases of Florence
fennel, which belongs to a completely
different botanical family, Apiaceae,
develop into a bulb-like structure that
grows above ground.

Onions *Allium cepa*

Onions, together with leeks, chives, shallots and garlic, are members of the *Allium* genus, which contains some 700 individual species of biennial and perennial plants. Like the ornamental alliums that are grown in flower borders, they will, if allowed to grow on, develop the typical flowerheads. They all, too, to varying degrees, have the characteristic onion smell, which is caused by sulphur-containing chemical compounds.

The large, round onions that are mainly used for cooking are traditionally grown from sets, which are small bulbs that have been grown from seed sown by commercial suppliers in the previous season. They are harvested at the end of the first season, when they are 1–2.5cm/½–1in across. The sets are then sold either loose or, more frequently these days, pre-packaged and sold by weight or, occasionally, number. The sets may be heat-treated by the supplier to kill the flower embryo, and this prevents bolting (prematurely running to seed).

Some types of onion can also be grown from seed if it is sown early enough in the year to give the onions a long growing season in which to develop. This usually means sowing under glass in midwinter, so that the plants can be put in the garden in mid-spring to grow on.

large and small red onions

brown onion

small brown onions

white onions

Pickling onions produce small, white bulbs. They are grown from seed sown close so that large bulbs do not develop, and they can be lifted about two months after sowing.

HISTORY

Onions are among the oldest of vegetables. They are known to have been grown in ancient Egypt more than 5,000 years ago, and it is likely they were eaten before then. The species is no longer found in the wild, but it may have originated in south-western Asia. The Romans took it with them as the empire extended into northern Europe, and by the Middle Ages it had become a staple vegetable in Britain. Christopher Columbus is believed to have taken the first onions to the American continent.

Onions have a huge number of culinary uses and can be eaten raw or cooked by frying, boiling or roasting. They are an essential ingredient of many soups and casseroles, and are the basis of a number of chutneys and pickles, as well as fresh foods such as salads.

VARIETIES
There are dozens of named cultivars to choose among, although there is generally a wider choice if you are growing from seed than from sets. Sets are usually more expensive than seed, and heat-treated sets are more expensive than untreated ones. If you do not have a greenhouse,

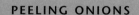
PEELING ONIONS

The easiest way to peel an onion is first to cut off the top and bottom, then slit the skin with a sharp knife and peel it off.

buy sets, and whenever space is limited it is more economical to plant sets. Onions are usually broadly grouped by colour: golden-brown, red and white. The main criteria for home-grown onions are flavour and storing qualities. Golden-skinned cultivars often store better than other kinds, but red and white onions have, respectively, sweeter and milder flavours and are ideal for adding to salads.

Among the best known and most widely available of the golden-skinned onions is 'Sturon', which should be grown from sets and harvested in autumn. 'Red Baron', which can be grown from sets or seed, is one of the best red onions. It tends not to bolt, and the lifted bulbs store well. 'Buffalo', which is best grown from autumn-

ABOVE The smallest onions are referred to as baby, button or pickling onions.

sown seed (although spring-sown seed will produce good-sized bulbs), is a reliable cropper and produces large, well-flavoured bulbs. A popular pickling onion is 'Paris Silver Skin', which produces evenly sized white onions.

NUTRITION
Onions contain volatile sulphur-containing compounds, which give the characteristic flavour and odour. They are a good source of beneficial phytochemicals, including vitamin C and small amounts of vitamin A, calcium, iron, potassium and fibre. They contain cycloallin, an anticoagulant, which helps protect against heart disease.

Shallots *Allium cepa* Aggregatum Group

Botanically, shallots are a variety of the familiar bulbing onion. Plants raised from seed produce a single bulb, like an onion, but plants raised from sets will develop into clumps of between eight and twelve lateral bulbs, and it is this characteristic that makes shallots immediately identifiable. They are variable in shape and size as well as in colour, which can range from yellow, through

shallots

shades of brown to red, and the flavour also varies from mild to strong.

Like onions, shallots can be grown from sets or seed. Sets are usually planted in late winter or early spring, while seed is sown in early to mid-spring. They are easy vegetables to grow and need little attention once the sets have put down roots or the seed has germinated. When space is at a premium, a row or two of shallots can be planted in the ornamental garden where, like garlic, they seem to keep pests and diseases at bay. They also store well.

HISTORY

Shallots are believed to have been used by the ancient Greeks and Romans, although the first record dates only from 12th-century France. It is thought that shallots (like leeks) were originally called scallions, after Ascalon (Ashqelon) in Israel, the place from where the Greeks thought the vegetable originated.

Like onions, however, it is more likely that shallots were native to areas in central or south-western Asia.

Shallots are widely used in cooking, especially in France, where they are often used in preference to onions. Because they tend to be smaller than onions, they

VARIETIES

'Atlantic' yellow skinned
'Delicato' red skinned
'Dutch Red' red skinned
'Dutch Yellow' yellow skinned
'Giant Red' red skinned
'Giant Yellow' yellow skinned
'Golden Gourmet' yellow skinned
'Hâtive de Niort' brown skinned
'Pikant' yellow skinned
'Sante' yellow skinned
'Success' red-brown skinned
'Topper' yellow skinned

are often more convenient when only a small quantity is required in a recipe. Although they lack the strong smell of onions and tend not to make the eyes water when they are chopped and sliced, the taste of cooked shallots is often more intense yet sweeter than that of

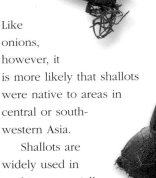

French shallots

If you are peeling a lot of shallots, it is easier if you first blanch them in boiling water. This is particularly helpful when peeling varieties that have tenaciously clinging tight skins that never seem to come off.

1 Cut off the neck of the shallots and cut a thin slice off the bottom – just enough to remove the roots, otherwise the shallots may fall apart in cooking.

2 Place the shallots in a bowl and add enough boiling water to cover them completely.

3 Leave in the water for about 3 minutes, drain, then slip the shallots out of their skins.

onions. Shallots are also popular for pickling, and the leaves can be used instead of chives, which they closely resemble.

ABOVE Shallots look much the same as small onions, but they generally have a milder, sweeter flavour.

VARIETIES

There are several named cultivars, although differences are more generally in size and colour than in flavour. French shallots tend to have a more pronounced taste and are worth seeking out. An established favourite is 'Hâtive de Niort', which has long, regularly shaped, dark brown bulbs with a good flavour and some resistance to the problem of rot.

'Atlantic' has golden-yellow skin and firm, crisp bulbs with a good flavour. This is an early-maturing shallot, so is a good choice in areas with a short growing season. 'Pikant' is another early-maturing, high-yielding cultivar, and the multiple bulbs keep well. 'Sante' needs warm soil to develop and should be grown only in gardens in sheltered areas and those with a long growing season. 'Dutch Yellow' has flattish bulbs with yellow skins that are often used for pickling.

NUTRITION

Shallots contain many beneficial phytochemicals, including vitamins A and C, calcium and iron.

Garlic *Allium sativum*

A very individual form of onion, garlic is characterized by its distinctive smell and flavour. It is widely used throughout the world for cooking and medicinal purposes and has been for thousands of years. It is thought to have originated in central Asia, but it can no longer be found in the wild. Even in cultivation it has ceased to set seed, and existing cultivars are thought to be very old indeed.

Garlic forms a bulb made up of numerous individual cloves. There are several different cultivars available worldwide, but they are broadly similar, the

main differences being taste and pungency. The skins are usually white but can be tinged to a lesser or greater extent with purple. The only other differences are the size and number of cloves, hardiness and storage qualities. Garden-grown garlic is often bigger and more pungent than purchased bulbs.

HISTORY

Garlic is first known to have been grown in around 3200 BC in ancient Mesopotamia. Inscriptions and models of garlic found in the pyramids of ancient Egypt testify to the fact that garlic was not only an important foodstuff but that it had ceremonial significance as well. The Greeks and Romans likewise believed garlic to have magical qualities. Warriors would eat it for strength before going into battle, gods were appeased with gifts of garlic, and cloves of garlic were fastened round the necks of babies

young, new-season or wet garlic

to ward off evil. Hence, vampire mythology has ancient precedents.

The Greeks and Romans also used garlic for its therapeutic qualities. Not only was it thought to be an aphrodisiac but also it was believed to be good for eczema, toothache and snake bites.

Although garlic found its way all over Europe – vats of butter strongly flavoured with garlic

garlic, with individual cloves

garlic stored in a bag

ABOVE A string of pink-skinned garlic.

which date back 200–300 years have been found by archaeologists working in Ireland – fundamentally, its popularity today derives from our liking for Mediterranean, Indian and Asian food, in which garlic plays an important part.

VARIETIES

Garlic is usually sold as unnamed bulbs, although you might find one or two named cultivars in some seed merchants' catalogues. It is possible to plant the cloves from a bulb bought from a greengrocer or farmers' market, and these will usually shoot and grow on. Bulbs bought from supermarkets are likely to have been treated and may fail to sprout altogether or, even if they do, may produce distorted or diseased leaves.

Among the named cultivars look out for 'Thermidrome', which is an established variety from the south of France. It will produce large, white bulbs containing about 10 cloves, and despite its origins it will do well in cool areas. Another cultivar from France is 'Printanor', which has pink, well-flavoured cloves. The bulbs keep well when lifted and have been shown to have good resistance to disease. 'Long Keeper', which develops large bulbs from autumn-planted cloves, is a good choice for gardens in cooler areas. Whether it is planted in autumn or spring 'Cristo' produces large, strongly flavoured bulbs. Elephant garlic produces larger than average bulbs, but the cloves do not have a particularly strong flavour.

PEELING GARLIC

The easiest way to peel garlic is to place it on a chopping board and use the blade of a wide-bladed knife flat to crush the clove.

1 Lay the blade of a knife flat on the clove and press down firmly on the blade with your fist or the heel of your hand, breaking the skin of the garlic.

2 The skin will then peel off easily. This also bruises the garlic, which allows the flavour to come out.

CRUSHING GARLIC

To attain a much stronger flavour, crush the garlic rather than chopping it.

Crush the garlic in a mortar with a pestle or, alternatively, crush it on a chopping board with the flat blade of a knife to make a paste. Adding a few flakes of sea salt to the garlic will make crushing much easier.

Easier still, press the peeled clove through a specially designed garlic press or crusher.

NUTRITION

Garlic is an excellent source of beneficial phytochemicals, including vitamins A and C, calcium and iron. Like other alliums, garlic contains allins, which may offer protection against cancer and heart disease, and raw garlic is an important source of sulphur compounds, which can lower the levels of cholesterol and triglycerides in the blood. It is also used externally to clear up skin complaints, such as acne and fungal infections.

Spring onions *Allium cepa*

Spring or salad onions (scallions) are non-bulbing forms of the normal onion, *Allium cepa*. They are eaten when the small bulbs are little more than a slight swelling at the base of the stem, which is generally about eight weeks after sowing. The leaves are usually a bright, fresh green, and the bulb and base of the stem are white.

Spring onions of all types can be used in cooked dishes, but they are more often eaten raw in salads. The leaves can be used in the same ways as chives, and the onions themselves are often used as a garnish, either chopped or whole.

ABOVE Bulb spring onions (scallions) are the best ones to use for grilling whole or for cooking in dishes such as Chinese stir-fries, or deep-frying whole in batter.

HISTORY

Like the large, bulbing onions of which they are a form, spring onions originated in central and south-western Asia. They are called spring onions simply because that is when they are usually ready to eat.

The perennial or biennial *A. fistulosum* (Welsh onion) is similar to the spring onion, although it is a completely different species. It produces cylindrical bulbs and hollow leaves, similar to chives. In fact, it has little to do with Wales and has been introduced to the West only recently, although it has been in cultivation in China since prehistoric times.

It found its way to the West by way of Russia in the early 17th century, possibly picking up its name from the German word *welsch*, which means Latin or southern. Bunching onions are similar and have developed from the Welsh onion; they can be treated as annuals, like spring onions, or cultivated as perennials, like Welsh onions.

VARIETIES

'Guardsman' is a popular choice, having a slightly sweet flavour and tender flesh. It has some resistance to white rot and tends not to develop a bulb, even when it is left in the ground to grow on. The perennial 'Ishikura', a form of Japanese bunching onion, produces stems that have little or no bulbing and if left to grow on in the garden

spring onions (scallions)

will form multi-stemmed clumps. It stays white and slim, and the onions can be harvested when they are pencil thin, or they can be left to grow on until they are as thick as carrots. 'Santa Claus' is similar to 'Ishikura', but it has intriguing reddish-pink stems and bright yellow-green leaves. If plants are left to grow on, they will continue to develop until they are as thick as leeks but will remain tender and sweet flavoured. The coloration can be intensified by earthing (hilling) up. 'Summer Isle', a Japanese bunching onion, has an exceptionally sweet flavour and is a good choice for adding to stir-fries as well as to salads; sow in succession for crops from summer until autumn. One of the oldest and

also one of the most widely available cultivars is the quick-growing 'White Lisbon', which should be sown successively to give spring onions over a long period in summer; it produces a short white stem and a pronounced round bulb. There is a winter-hardy form of this cultivar, which can be sown in autumn to give an early crop in spring. 'Winter White Bunching' can also be sown in late summer for cropping in mid- to late spring. 'Redmate', which is normally grown as a regular onion and left in the garden to develop into a bulb, can be treated as a spring onion when it is young. The bright red bulbs are especially attractive in salads.

ABOVE Slender spring onions are excellent in salads, whether left whole or chopped into fine slices.

NUTRITION

Like other vegetables in the allium family, spring onions are a good source of beneficial phytochemicals. They contain vitamin C, as well as moderate amounts of vitamin A, calcium, iron, potassium and fibre.

BELOW The succulent green tops of spring onions, as well as the white parts, are good both raw and cooked.

MAKING SPRING ONION TASSELS

Make a series of short, lengthways cuts at each end of the onions using a sharp knife or kitchen scissors to produce a neat tassel effect. Make sure you leave at least 2.5cm/1in of onion uncut in the centre.

Chill the spring onions in iced water for 30–45 minutes until the ends curl.

Leeks *Allium porrum*

Although they are closely related to the familiar bulbing onion, leeks do not develop such a pronounced basal swelling, and they do not have the same pungent flavour and distinctive smell as the other culinary members of the genus. They consist of cylinders of tightly wrapped leaves, which are white where they are blanched by being earthed (hilled) up, and green above, where they are exposed to the light. The cylinders are about 25cm/10in long and 2cm/¾in in diameter. The white section is the part that is used in the kitchen. Unlike other culinary onions, which are used mainly as flavourings, leeks are used as a vegetable in their own right, when they can be braised, boiled or simmered. They are also an essential ingredient in some traditional soups, including cock-a-leekie and vichyssoise, as well as being added to a wide range of stews and other dishes.

HISTORY

Like most types of onion, leeks have been grown for centuries, probably developing from *A. ampeloprasum* (Levant garlic), which is native to the Near East and countries around the Mediterranean. They were grown in ancient Egypt from about 2000 BC and were also eaten throughout the Greek and Roman periods. There is some evidence that they were enjoyed in Britain during the Dark Ages, but there are few mentions during the Middle Ages, and evidence suggests that between the 16th and 18th centuries leeks were not a fashionable food. Rural communities probably continued to plant and enjoy leeks, which will produce a substantial crop in a range of climatic conditions.

The leek has been the national emblem of Wales for hundreds of years. Its connections with that country arose because Welshmen were said to have worn leeks in their hats when their king, Cadwaladr, led them into battle against the Saxons in the 1st century AD. The leeks were to distinguish them from their enemies. In addition, many place names in England, including Leckhampstead in Buckinghamshire and Leighton Buzzard in Bedfordshire, are derived from the word leek. Leeks are popular with exhibition growers, who compete to produce the largest specimens.

leeks

VARIETIES
Autumn
'Albinstar'
'Autumn Giant Startrack'
'Autumn Mammoth-Argenta'
'Elephant'
'Pancho'
Mid-season
'Carentan'
'Cortina'
'Grenvilliers-Splendid'
'King Richard'
Winter
'Alaska'
'Giant Winter-Cantalina'
'Giant Winter-Royal Favourite'
'Giant Winter-3'
'Kajak'
'Musselburgh'
'Wila'
'Yates Empire'

TRIMMING AND CLEANING LEEKS

1 Trim off most of the loose green leaves, cutting at the point where the layers begin to get tighter. Discard any loose green leaves but, unless the recipe specifies the white part of the leek only, do not discard the green part of the bulb.

2 Trim off the excess root. Discard one or two outer layers of the leek, which are tough, fibrous and quite likely to have been damaged.

3 Make a slit starting about 2.5cm/1in from the base of the leek to the top, cutting through to the centre. Carefully wash the leek under cold running water, fanning out the layers with your fingers to make sure you wash away all the dirt. Hold the leek so that the water runs from the base to the top, so dirt will not be washed back into the layers of leaves.

ABOVE Baby leeks are good for serving whole. Steam, then brown in a hot griddle pan to bring out their flavour.

VARIETIES

A wide range of cultivars is available, but there is little difference in flavour among them. Some forms, especially those with blue leaves, such as the French heirloom cultivar 'Bleu de Solaise', are hardier than others, and some mature earlier. Some cultivars are sold specially for people who want large leeks for the show bench, although it must be said that flavour and texture are not high on the list of attributes of these rather specialized cultivars.

One of the longest established cultivars is the hardy 'Musselburgh', which has been grown since at least the 1820s. It is tolerant of a range of conditions and reliably produces good-sized, flavoursome

SLICING LEEKS

Cut across the width of the leek in the thickness you require.

When stir-frying, cut across the leek obliquely in a series of diagonal cuts. This exposes a larger surface area of the central portion of the leek to the heat, ensuring that it cooks quickly.

stems. 'King Richard' develops long, slim stems that do not need earthing up and that slice neatly without collapsing. It is a fairly quick grower, and early sowings will give a crop in early summer, while later sowings give an autumn crop, which can be kept for winter use. 'Giant Winter-Royal Favourite' is an attractive cultivar producing good-sized stems. It is a late variety and a very hardy one that stands the winter well.

NUTRITION

Leeks are a good source of vitamin C. Like other alliums, they contain allins, which are believed to offer protection against heart disease.

TYPES OF BULB VEGETABLES   **19**

Chives *Allium schoenoprasum*

This low-growing, hardy perennial, with narrow, tubular, rather grass-like leaves, is one of the basic culinary herbs that few gardeners will want to be without. Not only are chives invaluable in the kitchen, but their attractive pale purple to pink flowerheads are also a wonderful addition to the ornamental garden. Chives can be easily grown from seed in the flower border and are excellent additions to a potager or decorative kitchen garden. They are also neat enough to use as an edging to a path or plot.

An important culinary herb, chives have a more subtle flavour than their larger cousins in the onion family. The chopped leaves, which may be used as a flavouring or garnish, can be added to a wide

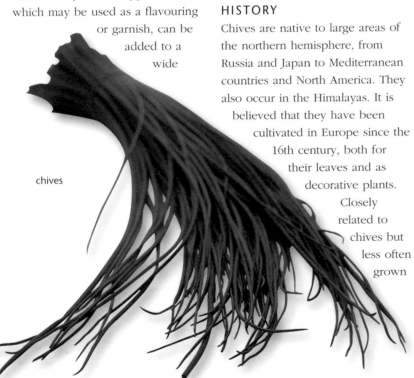

chives

range of dishes, including salads, soups and sauces, and they are frequently used to accompany egg and potato dishes. The flowerheads, but not the flower stalks, are also edible and can be added as a garnish to salads or other dishes.

HISTORY

Chives are native to large areas of the northern hemisphere, from Russia and Japan to Mediterranean countries and North America. They also occur in the Himalayas. It is believed that they have been cultivated in Europe since the 16th century, both for their leaves and as decorative plants. Closely related to chives but less often grown

ABOVE Chinese chives may be chopped and used in stir-fries.

is *A. scorodoprasum* (rocambole, sand leek). Rocambole has a more pronounced flavour, not dissimilar to garlic, and in summer it bears pink-purple flowers.

The clump-forming perennial *A. tuberosum* (Chinese chives, garlic chives) produces flat, grass-like leaves, which have a flavour midway between garlic and chives, and, like chives, they have attractive flowerheads that can be used in salads.

The interesting ornamental hardy perennial *A. cepa* var. *proliferum* (tree onion, Egyptian onion) produces bulbils at the top of the stem, instead of flowers; use the bulbs as you would shallots.

ABOVE Chives can be grown indoors in a container to give a year-round supply.

VARIETIES

Chives for culinary purposes are not generally sold as named cultivars, although you sometimes find plants labelled as having thin or thick leaves. Some cultivars have been developed, however, and these are usually distinguished by the flower colour, emphasizing the decorative rather than edible role of these plants, although the leaves of all can be used in the kitchen. The vigorous 'Forescate', which grows to 60cm/24in tall with a spread of about 8cm/3in, is one of the best known and most widely available; the flowers are a bright purple-pink. There is an attractive, naturally occurring white-flowered form, *A.* var. *sibiricum*, and the flowers of 'Pink Perfection' and 'Black Isle Blush' are deep pink.

NUTRITION

Because they are milder than other members of the onion family, chives are rarely used medicinally, although they do act as a stimulant and digestive. They contain

BELOW Chive flowers have a mild onion flavour and are pretty added to salads.

ABOVE Chinese chives have a flavour that is a mixture of garlic and chives.

CUTTING CHIVES

1 Hold a bunch of chives in your hand, snip the bunch level at one end with kitchen scissors, then snip off the amount you require.

2 Cut straight across to form little rings, or obliquely to form slanting chives.

Florence fennel *Foeniculum vulgare* var. *dulce*

The annual Florence fennel or sweet fennel is a variety of the herb fennel (*F. vulgare*), and it produces the same pretty, feathery fronds as the herb. However, it is distinguished from the herb by the fleshy base to the stems. It is smaller growing than the herb, reaching 60–75cm/24–30in high and with a spread of about 45cm/18in. The herb, on the other hand, can get to heights of 1.5m/5ft.

Florence fennel is grown for the edible bulbous swelling at the base of the stalks, but other parts of the plant can be eaten. The leaves can be used in the same way as the herb leaves for flavouring and garnishes, and the seeds are used for their aniseed flavour.

Florence fennel bulb

VARIETIES

'Argo'
'Cantino'
'Di Firenze' ('Sweet Florence')
'Dover'
'Fino'
'Herald'
'Mammoth Perfection'
'Rudy'
'Selma'
'Sirio'
'Tardo'
'Zefo Fino'

Florence fennel also makes a good foliage plant and is often grown just for its decorative, finely cut foliage, which has a light, airy quality. The main vegetable cultivars have bright green foliage, but some perennial forms of the herb have attractive bronze leaves. The plants need reliably moist, rich soil, when they will grow fast, but if they suffer any checks, such as drought or sudden changes of temperature, they are likely to bolt and run to seed before the bulb has formed.

The bulbous part that is eaten consists of the overlapping, swollen bases of the leaves. To cook Florence fennel trim off the leaves, cutting close to the bulb, and wash off any soil that may be lodged among the leaf stalks at the top of the bulb. The bulbs can be eaten raw in salads, as a crisp, aniseed-flavoured alternative to celery, or boiled and served as an accompaniment for chicken or, traditionally, fish.

HISTORY
Although its common name is Florence fennel, this plant is believed to have originated in the Azores. Nevertheless, in the early 18th century it was introduced to Britain from Italy, where it has been in cultivation for many centuries. Italy is still the main centre of production, and it is only recently that it has been widely grown in gardens.

Florence fennel with leaves attached

RIGHT The bulb of Florence fennel is actually composed of the swollen leaf stalks.

VARIETIES

Although several named cultivars have been developed, there is little to choose among them, and your choice will most likely be determined by the types available from your supplier. In cold areas it is worth searching for 'Précoce d'Eté', which is one of the hardiest forms. Sow it when the soil is warm (in late spring or early summer) and harvest it as soon as the bulb forms. It develops sweet-tasting bulbs with a distinct taste of liquorice.

'Mammoth Perfection' (sometimes sold as 'Perfection') develops large, white bulbs. It is less likely to bolt than some

ABOVE This row of well-grown, healthy-looking Florence fennel is of a cultivar called 'Dover'.

cultivars and tolerates most soil types. The bulbs have a subtle aniseed flavour. 'Cantino', 'Rudy' and 'Zefo Fino' will produce fairly large bulbs, and none of these cultivars will bolt. The cultivar 'Selma' is not widely available but, if you can track it down, it will reward you with large bulbs. 'Sirio' and 'Romy' are so similar that they may simply be regional names for the same plant. Whatever its name, this is a fast-growing, early-maturing plant, producing large, round bulbs. 'Di Firenze' is slightly smaller than 'Sirio' but otherwise very much the same.

NUTRITION

The bulbs are made up of about 95 per cent water. They are a good source of potassium and a number of minerals, carotene, vitamins E and B complex and a small amount of vitamin C.

PREPARING FENNEL

1 Cut off the stalks and remove any tough outer leaves (these can be used for a stock). Very young, tender bulbs may need little removed.

2 The bulb can be cooked whole, but when used raw in salads it needs to be thinly sliced or grated.

planning and
preparation

All vegetables will do best when they are grown in soil that has been thoroughly prepared and that suits their individual requirements. To give all these vegetables the best possible start and to ensure that they crop well, it is necessary to identify the type of soil in your garden and then to improve it through the regular addition of well-rotted compost or manure, through cultivation and through the removal of annual and perennial weeds.

Types of soil

Bulb vegetables can be grown in most types of ground, although they will do best in fertile but not freshly manured soil. Make sure that the soil is not only well-drained and moisture-retentive but also rich in nutrients. It is important that the soil does not dry out: these plants need a regular supply of moisture so that they do not bolt.

Identifying what type of soil you have in your garden is the first step towards providing the conditions they need. There are simple kits available for testing pH (acidity) and nutrient levels. To determine the structure, rub some moist soil between your fingers. A clay soil holds together well and can be rolled into a sausage shape – heavier clay will roll more thinly. Loam or silt will cohere but not press into shapes so easily. Sandy soil feels gritty and will not stick together.

CLAY SOIL

This type of soil can be difficult and heavy to work, and the particles cling together, making the soil sticky. Clay soil compacts easily, forming solid lumps that roots find hard to penetrate and making it difficult to dig. Try not to walk on clay soil when it is wet, which will compact the soil even more. In addition, clay soil is slow to drain in wet weather, but, when it is dry, it can set like concrete. It can also be cold and slow to warm up in spring, making it unsuitable for early crops. On the other hand, clay soil is slow to cool down in autumn, and it can be easily improved by the addition of well-rotted compost or manure and made easier to handle by the incorporation of grit. It is usually rich, and the hard work involved in the initial stages of improving it will pay off in the long term.

pH VALUES

1.0	extremely acid
4.0	maximum acidity tolerated by most plants
5.5	maximum acidity for reasonable vegetables
6.0	maximum acidity for most fruit and vegetables
6.5	optimum for the best fruit and vegetables
7.0	neutral, maximum alkalinity for good fruit and vegetables
7.5	maximum alkalinity for reasonable vegetables
8.0	maximum tolerated by most plants
14.0	extremely alkaline

SANDY AND SILTY SOIL

Soils high in sand and silts are composed of large grains that allow water to pass through them quickly, and this speedy passage of water through the soil tends to

WORKING IN ORGANIC MATTER

1 In an established garden, there is no need to dig deeply every year. Well-rotted organic matter can be added to the soil by spreading it over the surface.

2 Lightly work the organic material into the top layer of soil with a fork. There is no need for full-scale digging because worms will take the humus down.

TESTING THE SOIL FOR NUTRIENTS

1 Collect the soil sample 5–8cm/2–3in below the surface. Take a number of samples, and test each one separately.

2 With this kit, mix one part of soil with five parts of water. Shake well in a jar, then allow the water to settle.

3 Draw off some of the settled liquid from the top few centimetres (about an inch) for your test.

4 Carefully transfer the solution to the test chamber in the plastic container, using the pipette supplied.

5 Select a colour-coded capsule (one for each nutrient). Put the powder in the chamber, replace the cap and shake.

6 After a few minutes, compare the colour of the liquid with the shade panel of the container.

leach (wash) out nutrients, so that sandy soils are often rather poor as well as dry. However, they can be quick to warm up in spring, making them ideal for early crops. Silty soil contains particles that are more clay-like in texture than those found in sandy soils, and they hold more moisture and nutrients. Both types of soil are easy to improve and are not difficult to work. Sand does not compact as clay does, although it is still not good practice to walk on beds, but silty soil is susceptible to the impact of feet. Adding well-rotted organic material will make both types more moisture-retentive.

LOAM

This type of soil is a combination of clay and sandy soils, with the best characteristics of both. It tends to be both free-draining and also moisture-retentive. Although this may seem to be a contradiction in terms, it means that the soil is sufficiently free-draining to allow excess water to drain away easily, and waterlogging is unlikely to be a problem, but it is not too prone to drying out completely. This means that both water and air are freely available to the plants' roots, enabling them to take up the nutrients they need. Loamy soil is the ideal for which most gardeners strive.

ACID AND ALKALINE SOILS

Soils are also sometimes classified by their acidity or alkalinity. Those that are based on peat (peat moss) are acid; those that include chalk or limestone are alkaline. A scale of pH levels is used to indicate the degree of acidity or alkalinity. Neutral soil has a pH of 7; a pH lower than that indicates acidity, while a pH above 7 indicates an alkaline soil. Use one of the simple testing kits to check the soil in your garden. Take samples from several places, about 8cm/3in down – soil can vary within quite small areas – and simply follow the manufacturer's instructions on the packet.

Improving the soil

Once you have established the type of soil in your garden, perhaps the most important task in the garden is to improve and maintain the quality of the soil. Good-quality soil should be the aim of any gardener who wants to grow a range of vegetables – infertile or poorly structured soil will lead to poor yields and plants that are susceptible to pests and diseases.

IMPROVING SOIL QUALITY

The key to improving the soil in your garden is well-rotted organic material, especially garden compost, made from garden waste and vegetable waste from the kitchen, and farmyard manure. Both compost and manure are invaluable for improving the texture of the soil, and also contain significant amounts of nutrients.

IMPROVING SOIL FERTILITY

The fertility of the soil is much improved by the addition of organic material, but a quick boost can also be achieved by adding an organic fertilizer, spreading it over the surface and then raking it in.

It is important that such material is well rotted. If it is still in the process of rotting down when it is applied to the soil it will extract nitrogen from the soil as it continues to break down. This is, of course, the opposite of what the gardener wants – the aim is to add nitrogen to the soil. A good indicator that the material has broken down is that it is odourless. Even horse manure is free from odour once it has rotted down. Some bought-in materials contain undesirable chemicals, but these will be removed if the material is stacked and allowed to weather. Bark and other shredded woody materials may contain resins, for example, while animal and bird manures may contain ammonia from urea. These chemicals will evaporate or be converted during weathering.

REDUCING SOIL ACIDITY

The acidity of the soil can be reduced by adding lime some weeks before planting and working it in with a rake. Check the soil with a soil testing kit to see how much lime is required.

Although some crops can be grown on freshly manured ground, onions should be planted only in soil that was manured for a previous crop. In a crop rotation scheme, this will usually mean growing them where brassicas were grown the previous year.

DIGGING IN

When vegetables are grown in a dedicated part of the garden, the best way to apply organic material is to dig it in so that it is incorporated into the soil. If possible, double dig the bed, adding organic material all the way to the bottom of both spits. This will help the soil to conserve moisture and supply nutrients where they are needed, which is down around the roots. It will also encourage the roots to delve deeply, so that the plants are well anchored in the soil, rather than remaining on the surface where easy water can be obtained from rainfall and the watering can. The deeper the roots go, the more consistent will be the plant's water supply, and the plant will grow at a regular pace rather than in unproductive fits and starts. This will help to prevent alliums from bolting.

TOP-DRESSING

Once the ground has been planted, it is best not to dig around the plants, since this is likely to damage their roots. Organic matter can still be added, however, simply by spreading it on the surface of the soil around the plants. A layer 10cm/4in deep will be slowly worked into the soil by earthworms and other soil dwellers, and the dressing will also act as a mulch, protecting the ground from drying out as well as preventing weed seeds from germinating. Make sure that the top-dressing is free from weed seeds, or this last benefit will be lost, but hoeing off any weeds as they appear should not be too difficult. When garden soil has been thoroughly dug and plenty of organic matter added at the depth of one or two spades, many gardeners prefer not to dig the soil again. Instead, they apply a deep annual mulch. Applying a loose mulch such as chipped bark or cocoa shells will help to keep down weeds and conserve moisture in the ground. Grass clippings, if not applied too deep, are also a very good mulch.

WORKING ON WET SOIL

It is best to avoid working on wet soil, but sometimes it is necessary. To ensure that the soil is not compacted and its structure destroyed, it is advisable to work from a plank of wood.

IMPROVING SOIL STRUCTURE

1 One of the best ways to improve the structure of the soil is to add as much organic material as you can, preferably when the soil is dug. For heavy soils, this is best done in the autumn.

2 If the soil has already been dug, well-rotted organic material can be worked into the surface of the soil with a fork. The worms will complete the task of working it into the soil.

AMENDING THE SOIL'S PH

Alliums prefer a soil pH of 6–7. If you find that your soil has a pH below 5.5, which indicates acid conditions, you can adjust the pH upwards by adding lime to the soil. Ordinary lime (calcium carbonate) is the safest form to use. Quicklime (calcium oxide) is the strongest and most caustic, but it may cause damage and must be used with great care. Slaked lime (calcium hydroxide), which is quicklime with water added, is not as strong as quicklime and is easier to handle. Choose a windless day, wear protective clothing and follow the supplier's instructions about quantities to the letter. Do not try to overcompensate for an acid soil by adding more lime than is recommended as this may lead to nutrient deficiency. Do not add lime at the same time as manure because this will release ammonia, which can damage plants. Do not

sow or plant in the ground for at least a month after liming the soil. Mushroom compost, which is rich in lime, can be used instead.

It is more difficult to reduce the pH levels of alkaline soils. The traditional method was digging in peat (peat moss), but not only does it break down quickly and need to be continually replaced, but the collection of peat is now regarded as environmentally unacceptable. In any case, most soils tend to be slightly acid because calcium is continually leached out by rainfall, and most organic manures tend to be slightly acid and will help to reduce pH levels. Leaf mould, especially when it is made from pine needles, is also acid. If the soil in your garden is too alkaline for cultivating these vegetables, consider using raised beds, which you can fill with topsoil that is more suitable for vegetables, bought in from elsewhere.

Compost

This is a valuable material for any garden, but it is especially useful in the fruit and vegetable garden. It is free, apart from any capital cost required in installing compost bins, and these should last for many years, so the overall cost should be negligible. A little effort is required, but this is a small price to pay for the resulting gold dust.

THE PRINCIPLE

In making compost, gardeners emulate the natural process in which a plant takes nutrients from the soil, dies and then rots, so the nutrients return to the ground. In the garden, waste plant material is collected, piled in a heap and allowed to rot down before being returned to the soil as crumbly, sweet-smelling, fibrous material.

Because it is kept in a heap, the rotting material generates heat, which encourages it to break down more quickly. The heat also helps to kill pests and diseases, as well as any weed seed in the compost. The balance of air and moisture is important; if the heap is too wet it will go slimy, but if it is too dry it will not decompose. The best balance is achieved by having some ventilation, but protecting the compost from rain, and by using a good mixture of materials.

RIGHT Good compost is dark brown, crumbly and has a sweet, earthy smell, not a rotting one.

If you have a good, well-balanced collection of materials in your compost heap, it should take about three months to break down, although many gardeners like to leave it for at least six months before adding it to the garden.

THE COMPOST BIN

Gardeners always seem to generate more garden waste than they ever thought possible and never to have enough compost space, so when planning your bins, make sure you have enough. The ideal aim is to have three: one to hold new waste, one that is in the process of breaking down, and a third that is ready for use.

Bins are traditionally made from wood (often scrap wood), and because these can be hand-made to fit your space and the amount of material available, this is still the best option. Sheet materials, such as corrugated iron, can also be used. Most ready-made bins are

ABOVE A range of organic materials can be used, but avoid cooked kitchen waste and any perennial weeds. Clockwise from top left: kitchen waste, weeds, shreddings and grass clippings.

made of reinforced black or green plastic, and although these work perfectly well, they may be too small for a large garden.

You can make compost in a bin the size of a dustbin (trash can), but if you have room, one holding a cubic metre/35 cubic feet, or even bigger, will be much more efficient, since a bigger bin will get much hotter. The simplest bin can be made by nailing together four wooden pallets to form a box. If the front is made so that the slats are slotted in to form the wall, they can be removed as the bin is emptied, making the job of removing the compost easier.

MATERIALS

Most garden plant waste can be used for composting, but do not include perennial weeds. Weed seeds will be killed if the compost heats up really well, but it is safest not to include them. You could have a separate bin for anything that contains seeds because the compost can then be used for permanent plantings such as trees. If the compost never comes to the surface, seeds will not germinate. Woody material, such as hedge clippings, can be used, but shred it first. Kitchen vegetable waste, such as peelings and cores, can be used, but avoid cooked vegetables and do not include meat, which will attract rats and other vermin.

TECHNIQUE

Placing a few branches or twiggy material in the bottom of the bin will help to keep the contents aerated. Put in the material as it becomes available, but avoid building up deep layers of any one material, especially grass cuttings. Mix them with other materials.

To help keep the heap warm, cover it with an old carpet or a sheet of plastic. This also prevents rainwater from chilling the contents and swamping the air spaces. The lid should be kept on until the compost is needed.

Every so often, add a layer of farmyard manure if you can get it, because it will provide extra nitrogen to speed things up. Failing this, you can buy special compost accelerators. It is not essential to add manure or an accelerator, however – it just means waiting a couple of months longer.

Air is important, and this usually percolates through the side of the bin, so leave a few gaps between the timbers. If you use old pallets, these are usually crudely made, with plenty of gaps. The colder material around the edges takes longer to break down, so turn the compost around every so often. This also loosens the pile and allows air to circulate.

MAKING COMPOST

1 To make garden compost, place a layer of "browns" – straw, dry leaves and chipped wood are ideal – into the bin, to a depth of about 15cm/6in.

2 Begin a layer of "greens" – any green plant material, except perennial or seeding weeds. Fibrous or woody stems should be cut up small or shredded.

3 Add greens until you have a layer 15cm/6in thick. Mix lawn clippings with other green waste to avoid the layer becoming slimy and airless.

4 Kitchen refuse, including fruit and vegetable waste and crushed eggshells, can be added, but not cooked or fatty foods. Cover the heap.

5 Turn the heap occasionally. The speed of composting will vary, but when ready, the compost should be brown, crumbly and sweet-smelling.

Soil fertility

You cannot go on taking things out of the soil without putting anything back. In nature plants return the nutrients they have taken from the soil when they die. In the kitchen garden the vegetables are removed, and the chain is broken. Compost and other organic materials help to redress the balance, but to grow high-yielding crops, fertilizers may be needed as well.

WHAT PLANTS REQUIRE

The main foods required by plants are nitrogen (N), phosphorus (P) and potassium (K), with smaller quantities of magnesium (Mg), calcium (Ca) and sulphur (S). They also require small amounts of what are known as trace elements, including iron (Fe), boron (Bo) and manganese (Mn).

Each of the main nutrients tends to be used by the plant for one specific function. Thus nitrogen is concerned with plant growth and is used for promoting the rapid growth of the green parts of the plant. Phosphorus, usually in the form of phosphates, is used to create good root growth as well as helping with the ripening of fruits, while potassium, in the form of potash, is used to promote flowering and formation of good fruit and vegetables.

ABOVE To add nutrients naturally to the soil, rot down old plant material in a compost bin for up to six months, and then return it to the soil.

THE NATURAL WAY

The most natural way to add nutrients to the soil is to use compost and other organic matter. Such materials are important to the general structure of the soil, but they also feed it. Well-rotted farmyard manure and garden compost have been the main way that gardeners have traditionally fed their gardens. However, some gardeners, especially those in towns, may not have easy access to large quantities of these organic materials, or space to store them. Bought fertilizers, either organic or inorganic, can be a simple way of giving plants the nutrients they need.

Organic materials normally contains less of the main nutrients than concentrated fertilizers, but they are often strong in trace elements, and although they may not contain such a strong

ORGANIC FERTILIZERS

blood

bonemeal

seaweed meal

fish/blood/bone

concentration of nitrogen, they do release it over a longer period. Because of their other benefits, farmyard manure and garden compost are still the best all-round way of improving the soil, and also encourage earthworms and a healthy balance of micro-organisms.

ORGANIC FERTILIZERS

Concentrated fertilizers can be either organic or inorganic. Organic fertilizers are made from naturally occurring organic materials. Bonemeal (ground-up bones) is quite strong in nitrogen and phosphates, making it a good fertilizer to promote growth, especially at the start of a plant's life. Bonemeal also has the advantage that it breaks down slowly, releasing the fertilizer over a long period. When you apply bonemeal, you may want to wear gloves. Other organic fertilizers include fish, blood and bone (containing quick-release nitrogen and also phosphorus); hoof and horn (high in nitrogen); and seaweed meal (containing nitrogen and potassium). Because these are purely natural products, they are used by organic growers.

INORGANIC FERTILIZERS

These are fertilizers that have been made artificially, although they are frequently derived from natural rocks and minerals and the process may just involve crushing. They are concentrated and are usually soluble in water. This means that they are instantly available for plants and are useful for giving a plant a push when it is required. They do tend to wash out of the soil and need to be replaced. Some are general fertilizers, with equal proportions of nitrogen, phosphorus and potassium. Others are much more specific. Superphosphate, for example, is entirely used for supplying phosphorus; potash (potassium sulphate) provides potassium; and ammonium nitrate is added when nitrogen is required.

Increasing numbers of gardeners are turning against inorganic fertilizers, unaware that they may not be as artificial as is generally believed. Many are not classified as organic simply because they are not derived from living things. Nevertheless, it is their concentrated form and the fact that they can be readily washed from the soil that leads many gardeners to object.

SLOW-RELEASE FERTILIZERS

Some fertilizers are coated so they are released slowly into the soil. These are expensive in the short term, but because they do not leach away and do not need to be replaced as frequently, they save trouble and can provide a regular supply of nutrients to the plants over a long period. They are particularly useful for container planting, where constant watering is necessary (with its attendant rapid nutrient leaching).

INORGANIC FERTILIZERS

Growmore (not available in USA)

ammonium nitrate

potash

superphosphate

Digging the soil

Although it is a technique that is now being questioned by some gardeners, digging is still one of the main garden activities. It breaks up the soil, allowing the ingress of water and air, which are both important for plant growth. In addition, it also allows organic material to be incorporated deep down in the soil, right where the roots need it.

Digging enables you to remove weed roots – especially important on previously uncultivated ground – and it also helps bring pests to the surface, where many will die or be eaten by birds or other predators.

SINGLE DIGGING

The most frequently carried out method is single digging, and there are two ways, one informal and the other formal. The informal method is best used when the ground is quite loose; the gardener simply forks it over, turning it and replacing it in the same position, hardly using any trench at all. This process is often carried out on light or sandy soils.

Formal single digging is necessary on heavier soils and when there is organic material to be incorporated. First, a trench is dug across the width of the plot, and the earth from the trench is taken to the other end of the bed. Compost or farmyard manure is put into the bottom of the trench and then another trench is dug. The earth removed from the trench is put into the first trench to cover the

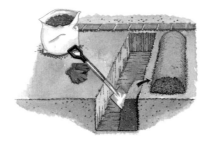

1 Start by digging a trench to one spade's depth across the plot, putting the soil from the first trench to one side to be used later in the final trench.

2 Put a layer of manure in the bottom of the trench. Dig out the next trench and cover the manure with earth taken from the second trench.

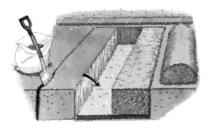

3 Repeat this process of adding manure to each trench and filling in with earth from the next, breaking up the soil as you go and keeping the surface even.

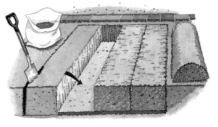

4 Continue down the length of the plot until you reach the final trench. This should be filled in with the earth taken from the first trench.

ABOVE After a winter exposed to the weather, most soils can be broken down into a fine tilth by using a rake. More recently turned soil may need to be broken down with a heavier hoe first.

organic material. This procedure is repeated down the length of the plot. When the final trench has been dug and organic material placed in it, it is refilled with the soil taken from the first trench.

Alternatively, the first trench can be dug so that it is two trenches wide. Organic material is put in the bottom as usual, and then the next trench is dug but the soil is spread over the bottom of the previous two trenches, only half-filling them. This is then covered with more organic material and then the fourth trench dug, filling up the

RIGHT For larger gardens with heavy soil, a rotavator (rototiller) will break down the soil into a fine tilth. Even a small one saves a lot of time, especially if the soil is too dry to break down with a rake.

first. Trenches three and four are treated in the same way, being filled first with the soil from trench five and then that from trench six.

DOUBLE DIGGING

Double digging is employed to break up the subsoil and is useful on any new plot of ground as well as when deep beds are being prepared. Dig the trench as before, taking the earth to the end of the

plot. Dig the subsoil in the bottom of the trench to the depth of a fork or spade, adding in organic material. Add more organic material on top and then dig the next trench, placing the soil into the first. Repeat until you reach

the end of the plot. Do not bring any subsoil up to the top.

MECHANICAL DIGGING

A mechanical rotavator (rototiller) can save time and effort on a large plot. One disadvantage is that it cuts up weed roots into small pieces, making them more difficult to remove by hand than with conventional digging.

BREAKING DOWN INTO A FINE TILTH FOR SOWING

The best time to dig a heavy soil is in the autumn, then the winter frosts and rain will break it down for you. If clay soils are dug in the spring and allowed to dry out too much, they are difficult to break down because the clods set like concrete. A mechanical rotavator makes breaking the soil down easier. Work on the soil when it is neither waterlogged nor completely dry, breaking it down, first with a large hoe and then with a rake. Shuffling along the surface with your feet will also help considerably, but do not do this if the ground is wet.

It is better to leave sandy soils until the spring because they do not need much breaking down. Raking the surface is usually all that is required.

Occasionally, the soil becomes too hard to break down. If this happens, water the soil well, leave it to dry slightly – so that it is no longer muddy – and then break it down. Alternatively, draw out a deep sowing row in the rough soil, fill it with potting compost (soil mix) and sow in this.

DOUBLE DIGGING

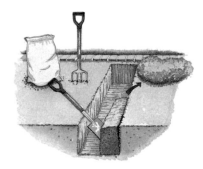

1 Dig a trench to one spade's depth, placing the soil to one side to be used later when filling in the final trench.

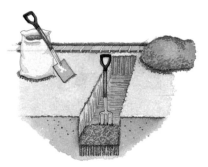

2 Break up the soil at the bottom of the trench, adding manure to the soil as you proceed.

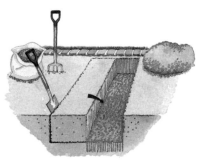

3 Dig the next trench, turning the soil over on top of the broken soil in the first trench.

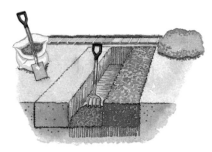

4 Continue down the plot, ensuring that subsoil from the bottom of the trenches is not mixed with topsoil.

Sowing and planting in the open

Leeks and onions are hardy plants that will benefit from the longest possible growing season, and seed can be sown outdoors from early spring. As long as the ground is not frozen or waterlogged, it is worth beginning to make a successional sowing, with others following at two- or three-week intervals to give crops over a long period.

PREPARING THE SOIL
To give the seeds a good start, prepare the soil carefully. Several weeks before you plan to sow, remove any weeds that have appeared and rake the soil to break it down into a fine tilth. Cloches or movable frames can also be used to warm up the soil and to prevent it from getting too wet in spring downpours. A floating mulch, such as horticultural fleece, black plastic or even sheets of newspaper, which can be held down with U-shaped lengths of wire or stones, will also help to warm up the soil. If the ground is dry, it is best not to cover it with anything that keeps rain off. Fleece and woven types of plastic will allow rain through, and fleece, since it also allows light through, can be left in place after the seed has been sown.

SELECTING SEED
Most of the seed that is available these days is of a high quality, especially when it comes from one of the major suppliers, and the rate of germination is usually good. Non-germination is usually due to a factor such as planting into ground that is too wet or too cold.

SOWING SEED

1 Draw out a shallow drill with the corner of a draw hoe, using a garden line to ensure that it is straight.

2 If the soil is dry, water along the length of the drill and allow it to drain before sowing seed.

3 Station sow the seed along the drill in groups of three, at the recommended distances for the variety.

4 Put a label at the end of the row clearly showing what is in the row. Put a stick or another label at the far end. Do this before filling in the drill.

5 Rake the soil into the drill over the seed. Gently tamp down the soil along the row with the flat of the rake and then lightly rake over.

6 If the soil is heavy and is difficult to break into a fine tilth, draw out the drill and then line it with potting compost (soil mix) before sowing.

GROWING ALLIUMS FROM SEED

ABOVE Alliums are fairly hardy plants, and small seedlings, growing outdoors, will survive a mild frost. Therefore, seed may be sown outdoors in mid- to late spring.

TRANSPLANTING SEEDLINGS

ABOVE When transplanting leeks, make holes with a dibber and drop the seedlings in. Water well; there is no need to fill with soil.

PLANTING SETS

ABOVE Plant sets in rows, firming them in gently. Required depths vary with the variety, and you can also plant slightly deeper in lighter soils.

Many gardeners like to save their own seed, especially if they are growing unusual or heritage varieties. Bought seed, however, is usually of F1 hybrids, which means that the seed is of first-generation plants, obtained by crossing two selected parents. The plants growing from such seed will be vigorous, uniform and, in the case of vegetables, high yielding. They might also show resistance to particular pests and diseases. The seed collected from such plants, however, will not necessarily come true to type.

SOWING SEED

The conventional way of sowing seeds is in rows, and this is generally a successful method for alliums. A length of garden twine will help you to keep the rows straight. If it is more convenient, you can also broadcast the seeds in a prepared bed. Cover the seeds with a depth of about 1cm/½in of soil, water well and label clearly.

PROTECTING SEED

Speed of germination can be increased by protecting each group of seeds with a cloche. Remove the cloche, just during the daytime at first, once the seed has germinated, and protect the tender young seedlings from slugs. This is best done by non-chemical means, since slug poisons will lead to birds and other predators being harmed by eating the dead slugs.

Newly sown seed and freshly cultivated ground is always attractive to birds, which will enjoy using the fine soil for dust baths, and many will also eat the seeds or seedlings. Protect the seeds by erecting wire-netting guards, or leave the cloches in place until the seedlings have grown large enough to withstand being pulled out by hungry birds. Wire guards are better when it is hotter.

TRANSPLANTING SEEDLINGS

Once the seedlings are large enough, dig them up and transplant them to their final growing position, spacing them according to the needs of the variety. Any spare seedlings can be used in salads. Water the transplanted seedlings in well.

PLANTING SETS

Sets are often an easier way to grow alliums, especially in cold areas, or in heavy soil, where seeds may not germinate readily. Plant the sets in rows, making holes with a dibber at the appropriate depth and spacing for the variety. Water in well. Keep the bed weeded by hand; alliums have shallow roots that are easily damaged by hoeing.

Sowing under glass

Germinating seeds under glass is more tedious and time-consuming than sowing direct into the ground, but raising plants in this way has its advantages. It allows the gardener to grow reasonably sized plants that are ready to set out as soon as the weather allows, stealing a march on those sown in the soil by about two weeks. If there are pest problems, such as slugs or birds, the plants are better able to resist them if they are well grown when they are planted out than if they have to fight for their life as soon as they emerge through the soil.

CONTAINERS

Seeds can be sown in a variety of containers. Traditionally they were sown in wooden trays or flats. Some gardeners prefer to make their own, claiming that they are warmer and that they can be made deeper than the purchased equivalents. Plastic trays have,

ABOVE A range of pots and trays is available for sowing seed. Clockwise from top left: individual cells, a half tray, plastic pots, a fibrous pot and fibrous modules.

however, generally replaced the wooden varieties. They can be made of rigid plastic for repeated use or thin, flimsy plastic, to be used only once before being thrown away. Often, however, only a few plants may be required, and it is rather wasteful to sow a whole or half tray. A 9cm/3½in pot may be sufficient.

Gardeners are increasingly using modular or cellular trays, in which one or two seeds are sown in a small cell. If both germinate, one is removed and the remaining seedling is allowed to develop without having to be pricked out. This method has the advantage of reducing root disturbance.

Even less root disturbance occurs if the seeds are sown in biodegradable fibrous modules. As soon as the seedling is big enough to be planted out, both pot and plant are inserted into the ground, and the pot allows the roots to grow through its sides into the surrounding earth.

SOWING IN POTS

Fill the pot with a good seed compost (soil mix), tap it on the bench, water, and sow from one to three seeds in each pot, depending on the size.

SOWING IN TRAYS

1 Fill the seed tray with seed compost and tamp it down lightly to produce a level surface. Water, allow to drain, then sow the seed thinly and evenly across the compost.

SOWING IN BLOCKS

Fill the cellular block with compost and tap it on the table to firm it down. Water, then sow one or two seeds in each cell. Cover with about 1cm/½in of compost.

2 Cover with a layer of about 1cm/½in compost, lightly firm down, water carefully and label. Labelling is very important because the seedlings of many vegetables look the same.

WATERING IN

Water the trays or pots by standing them in a shallow tray or bowl of water so that the water comes halfway up the container. Remove the tray or pot as soon as the surface of the compost begins to moisten, and allow to drain.

PROPAGATORS

Propagators are glass or transparent plastic boxes that help to keep the seed tray moist and in a warm atmosphere. Some models have cables in them so that the temperature can be controlled. Cheap alternatives can also be made simply by slipping the tray into a plastic bag and removing it when the seeds have germinated. Plastic jars can be cut down to fit over trays or pots.

USING A COLD FRAME

1 Once the trays or pots of pricked-out seedlings are ready to plant out, harden them off by placing in a cold frame which is opened a little wider each day but closed at night, to begin with.

USING A PROPAGATOR

1 Place the containers in a propagator. You can adjust the temperature of heated propagators like this. Seed packets should indicate the best temperature, but you may need to compromise if different seeds need different temperatures.

HEAT

A source of heat is useful for the rapid germination of seeds. It can be provided in the form of a heated propagator, but most seeds will germinate in a warm greenhouse or even within the house.

SOWING SEED

Fill the seed tray with a good-quality seed or potting compost (soil mix). Gently firm down and sow the seeds thinly on the surface.

2 Finally leave the lights of the cold frame off altogether so that the plants become accustomed to outside temperatures. Keep an eye on the weather and cover if frost is forecast.

2 This propagator is unheated and should be kept in a warm position in a greenhouse or within the house. Start opening the vents once the seeds have germinated so that they begin the hardening-off process.

Cover the seeds with about 1cm/½in of potting compost and firm down lightly. Water by placing the seed tray in a shallow bowl of water. Once the surface of the compost shows signs of dampness, remove the tray, let it drain, and place it in a propagator or plastic bag. A traditional alternative is to place a sheet of glass over the tray.

SUBSEQUENT TREATMENT

As soon as the seeds begin to germinate, let in air, and after a couple of days remove the cover altogether. If you are using a propagator, turn off the heat, open the vents over a few days and then remove the tray. Once the seedlings are large enough to handle, prick them out into trays, pots or modules. Make sure they are well spaced and keep them watered.

Before planting them out, harden them off in a cold frame, or by bringing them outside for gradually increasing periods of time each day.

Garden tools

To look in the average garden centre you would imagine that you need a tremendous battery of tools and equipment before you could ever consider gardening, but in fact you can start (and continue) gardening with relatively few tools and no equipment at all.

Tools are personal things, so one gardener may always use a spade for digging, no matter how soft the ground, whereas another would always use a fork as long as the ground was not too heavy. The type of hoe for certain jobs is another subject on which gardeners hold widely different opinions.

BUYING TOOLS

It is not necessary to buy a vast armoury of tools when you first start gardening. Most jobs can be done with a small basic kit. When you are buying, always choose the best you can afford. Many of the cheaper tools are made of pressed steel, which soon becomes blunt, will often bend and may even break. Stainless steel is undoubtedly the best, but tools made of this tend to be expensive. Ordinary steel implements can be almost as good, especially if you keep them clean. Avoid tools that are made of aluminium. Trowels and hand forks especially are often made of aluminium, but they wear down and blunt quickly and are not good value for money.

SECOND-HAND

A good way to acquire a collection of tools is to buy them second-hand. As well as usually being cheaper than new ones, they are often made of much better steel than cheap, modern ones and still retain a keen edge, even after

SOIL TESTERS

A range of soil testers are available. The most commonly used checks the acidity/alkalinity of the soil. It involves mixing soil samples with water and a chemical formulation and checking the colour against a chart. Electronic meters can also be used – they have a wand which is simply inserted into the soil. Other chemical-based tests check the nutrient levels. The balance can then be adjusted by adding lime or fertilizers to the soil.

many years' use. Another potential advantage is that, in the past, gardening tools were made with a much greater variation in design and size. If you go to buy a modern spade, for example, you will probably find that the sizes in the shop are all the same – designed for the "average" gardener. Old tools come in all shapes and sizes, and if you find modern tools uncomfortable to use

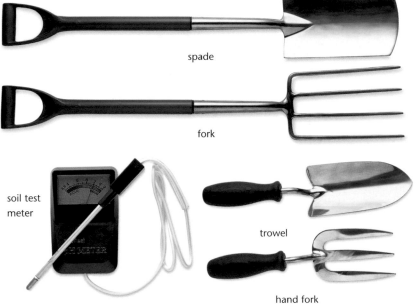

spade

fork

soil test meter

trowel

hand fork

gloves

you are more likely to find an old one that is made just for you.

Not all old tools are good by any means, of course, but by keeping an eye out and buying only good-quality ones you will end up with tools that will more than see you through your gardening career and at a relatively modest price. Look out for them at car boot sales (garage sales) and in rural junk shops (second-hand stores). Avoid antique shops where such tools are sold at inflated prices to be hung as decorations on the wall rather than to be used.

CARE AND MAINTENANCE

Look after your tools. If you do this they will not only always be in tip-top working condition but should last a lifetime. Scrape all the mud and any vegetation off the tools as soon as you have used them. Once they are clean, run an oily rag lightly over the metal parts. The thin film of oil will stop the metal from corroding. This not only makes the tools last longer but also makes them easier to use because less effort is needed to use a clean spade than one with a rough surface of rust.

In addition, keep the wooden parts of all tools clean, wiping them over with linseed oil if the wood becomes too dry.

Keep all blades sharp. Hang tools up if possible. Standing spades and hoes on the ground, especially if it is concrete, will blunt them over time. Keep them away from children.

EQUIPMENT

It is possible to run a vegetable garden with no mechanical aids at all. However, if you have grass paths, a lawn mower will, obviously, be more than useful – it will be essential. Hedge cutters, too, are useful, although hedges can be cut by hand much more easily than grass paths.

In the vegetable garden itself the only mechanical device that you may require is a rotavator (rototiller), which can be used for digging and breaking up the soil. This is far from essential, even in a large garden – after all, many gardeners enjoy digging – but it does make life easier if you want to break down a large area of heavy soil into a fine tilth.

Keep all your equipment maintained and serviced regularly, and always make sure you follow the manufacturer's safety instructions.

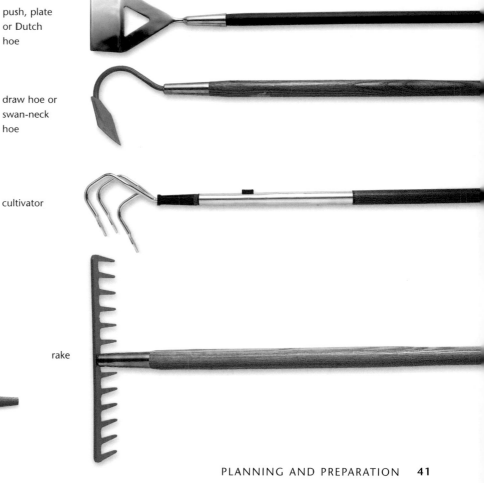

push, plate or Dutch hoe

draw hoe or swan-neck hoe

cultivator

rake

labels

dibber

Pests and diseases

The list of potential pests and diseases that can affect bulb vegetables can so alarm gardeners that they decide not to try growing these vegetables at all. This is a shame, because as long as the ground around them is kept well weeded and well fertilized, the healthy, vigorous plants will be able to fend off most problems. For some gardeners one of the most difficult aspects of controlling problems is to be completely ruthless about digging up and disposing of diseased crops – they should be thrown away or burned, not composted. It is far better to have a gap in the garden for a few months than to allow a disease or pest to become endemic.

Onions of all types, shallots and leeks suffer from many of the same pests and diseases. Many of the chemicals that were regularly recommended for garden use are no longer available, so avoid pests and diseases by practising crop rotation and good cultivation techniques and by weeding and watering regularly. Inspect plants as often as you can and remove and destroy any that show signs of insect infestation or disease so that problems do not spread to neighbouring plants and through the garden.

A MIXED GARDEN

One of the best ways to reduce pest and disease attacks is to grow a wide range of crops, mixed together. This means that any problem which only affects one type of plant will have less opportunity to become established.

Growing plenty of flowers, especially open, daisy-like ones such as marigolds and poached-egg plants (*Limnanthes douglasii*), will attract many beneficial insects such as hoverflies, which will help to reduce the population of aphids. Many gardeners grow such flowers alongside vegetables in the kitchen garden, which brightens up the area as well as serving a useful purpose. Growing a selection of flowering herbs, such as thyme, rosemary and marjoram, will also attract a wide range of insects. Alternatively, since alliums are attractive plants, you may wish to grow them amongst the flowers in the ornamental garden.

PESTS

Minute onion eelworms are the most serious pest. Infested plants become distorted, twisted or swollen (a problem often known as onion bloat), while the leaves become floppy and have a mealy appearance. The bulbs (if any are produced) will not keep. Remove any plants that appear to be infested as soon as you notice them. Crop rotation will help keep down the problem, but if you have lost plants to eelworms do not grow any alliums or any other susceptible plants (including all brassicas, as well as lettuce, turnips and swedes) in the same soil for several years to clear the ground.

LEFT All types of marigold will attract beneficial insects to the garden, and French marigolds (*Tagetes patula*) have been found to deter many insect pests, although it is unclear why; they may produce some substance the pests dislike.

RIGHT Poached-egg plants (*Limnanthes douglasii*) are one of the best flowers for attracting beneficial insects. They have a relatively short season; sow them successively for a longer flowering period.

ABOVE Snails have few friends among gardeners. They make holes in just about any part of a plant, often leaving it useless or even dead. They can be controlled by catching them in traps containing beer or upturned grapefruit skins. Alternatively, there are a variety of barriers and deterrents commercially available.

Onion fly affects onions and also sometimes leeks, shallots and garlic. The damage is done by the maggots, which eat the roots, causing the plants to collapse, and also the bulb tissue. Proprietary dusts can be used in the soil, but because the maggots feed inside the bulbs they will not be affected. Remove and burn any plants that appear to be infested. Onions grown from sets are often less susceptible.

Onion thrips feed on sap, and they cause the leaves on which they have been feeding to turn white-grey. They are a particular problem in hot, dry weather, and a severe infestation will stunt the plants' growth and may need control by appropriate sprays.

DISEASES

Downy mildew causes the leaves to turn grey, to wither and, eventually, to die back, and it is an especial problem in wet seasons. Preventive spraying and good crop rotation can help. Avoid the problem by spacing plants well and keeping down weeds. Do not try to store affected bulbs, which will, in any case, usually be found to be soft on lifting.

Rust affects all members of the *Allium* genus, but particularly leeks (it is sometimes known as leek rust). It causes reddish spots and streaks on the leaves, which may eventually turn yellow and die. Remove and burn all affected plants and practise regular crop rotation. Avoid planting leeks in nitrogen-rich soil.

All alliums are also susceptible to the fungal disease white rot, which causes the roots and base of the bulbs to rot. The affected tissue is covered with white fluff. Remove and burn affected plants and do

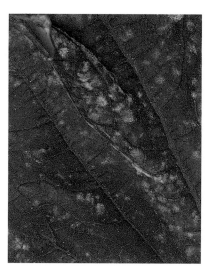

ABOVE Downy mildew is a fungal disease that appears as a grey coating over wilting leaves. It tends to thrive in warm, moist conditions.

not try to grow any member of the genus in the same soil for several years.

Stored onions can suffer from the fungal disease neck rot. Only store healthy, well-grown bulbs and leave them to dry before storing in a cool, well-ventilated place.

PHYSIOLOGICAL DISORDERS

Bolting (the premature production of flowers) can occur if watering has been erratic or if seed was sown too early. Cut off the shoot as soon as it is seen and allow the bulb to grow on, although they should be eaten rather than stored. Faulty root action, a cause of bolting, can also lead to splitting and bull neck.

LEFT Rust is one of the most serious diseases to affect alliums, and leeks are especially susceptible.

Growing organically

As increasing numbers of people become concerned about the levels of chemical insecticides, fertilizers and fungicides used to ensure that mass-produced vegetables look attractively uniform in size, shape and colour, growing vegetables organically is becoming ever more popular. Bulb and root vegetables can retain large amounts of chemicals, so growing them organically is especially worthwhile.

MAKING THE CHANGE

Many gardeners are deterred from abandoning all chemical aids because there can be no doubt that, at first, a garden run on organic-only lines does see a slight increase in the level of pests and diseases, especially those transmitted by insect pests. This is a temporary problem, however, and as soon as a good balance is established, the incidence of both pests and diseases will begin to fall. As the number of beneficial insects in a garden increases, insect pests are reduced. Natural predators, ranging from blue tits and hedgehogs to ladybirds (ladybugs) and lacewings, will thrive in an organic garden, but it will take some time for populations to become established and to build up to levels where they can be effective in controlling the levels of insect pests.

FEEDING THE SOIL

Rather than adding chemical fertilizers to the soil, organic gardeners add organic matter, such as well-rotted manure or garden compost, spent mushroom compost and seaweed, which have the added advantage of improving the texture of the soil. Worm compost, mostly derived from vegetable waste, is also highly fertile. Liquid comfrey, made by rotting down comfrey leaves in water and diluting the result 20:1, is a good source of nitrogen and phosphate. Along with seaweed extract, which contains trace elements, this will boost growth throughout the growing season.

If you test your soil and find that it is deficient in nutrients but you do not want to add a chemical formulation, choose from among the following to counter the

BELOW In a crop rotation system, alliums are best planted where brassicas were grown the previous year.

particular deficiency: bone meal, fish, blood and bone, hoof and horn, pelleted chicken manure, seaweed meal, rock phosphate, organic potash, ground limestone or dolomitic limestone and gypsum.

GREEN MANURES

Practising crop rotation, which is good practice whether your garden is organic or not, can mean that a section of the vegetable plot lies fallow for a season. Growing a green manure will both help maintain the structure of the soil and help to replace nutrients that have been lost to the previous crop. Grazing rye, for example, is useful for improving the structure of the soil, while clover can add to the soil's fertility by taking up nitrogen from the air. The green manure is sown, allowed to grow

and then simply dug back into the ground before it matures, where it decomposes, releasing the nutrients as it does so. Sowing a green manure is also a good way of preventing weeds from colonizing what would otherwise be bare soil.

BIOLOGICAL CONTROLS

Biological controls are increasingly used to control many common pests, although some are not suitable for outdoor use. Among the most useful is *Bacillus thuringiensis,* a bacterium that prevents caterpillars from eating, thereby effectively killing them. The bacterial spores, which produce a protein that is toxic to caterpillars, are sprayed on to the leaves of any vegetable that is susceptible to caterpillar damage. It does, however, kill all butterfly and moth caterpillars and must be applied with care. Its increasing use in genetically modified corn is, unfortunately, making it less effective in the US, where resistant varieties of pests have developed. It is still worth using in UK gardens, however.

Slugs are one of the main pests of all vegetables. Once the soil has reached a temperature over 5°C/41°F, nematodes can be watered into the soil, and these will infect and kill soil-dwelling slugs. The nematodes are completely harmless to children, wildlife and pets, and birds and hedgehogs can safely eat slugs after application.

Biological controls usually work best when the weather is warm. Introduce them as soon as the first

ABOVE A "lacewing hotel" provides an area where lacewings – whose larvae eat large quantities of aphids – can live.

signs of attack are noticed. Be patient and accept that there will be some damage before the biological agent takes effect. When you use biological controls there will always be some pests, which are essential for the predator to continue to breed, but the population will be reduced.

COMPANION PLANTING

Cottage gardeners often plant chives and garlic around rose and fruit bushes in the belief that they will help ward off fungal and bacterial attacks. In the vegetable garden, avoid planting onions and garlic near peas and beans, although they will do well with beetroot and chards, lettuces, strawberries, summer savory and tomatoes. Leeks do well with carrots, celery and onions.

cultivating
bulb
vegetables

Most bulb vegetables are easy to grow, provided you can create the right conditions for them. All of them like plenty of sun, and soil that is not too heavy. Even if the soil in your garden is really unsuitable, you should be able to achieve success by growing the crops in raised beds, filled with topsoil brought in from elsewhere. As long as you prepare the ground well, and weed and water regularly, you should be rewarded with a plentiful supply of delicious vegetables.

Growing onions

Onions should be planted in an open position in a light soil that has been manured during the previous autumn. They need a pH of 6–7.

Plant the sets out in early spring. Some types are heat-treated, which prevents them from bolting, and they can be planted out later, in mid- to late spring, when the soil is warmer. Plant them at 10cm/4in intervals in rows that are spaced about 30cm/12in apart. Plant with a dibber and cover the bulbs so that only the tips are showing.

Seed can be sown under glass in midwinter. Harden off and plant out in mid-spring. Alternatively, sow outside in spring. Sow Japanese onions directly in beds in late summer or plant out as sets in early autumn.

Keep the beds weed free by hand, not hoeing – onions have shallow roots. There is generally no need to water unless the summer is particularly dry.

CULTIVATION

Sets
Planting time: early spring (most varieties); early summer (overwintering varieties)
Planting distance: 10cm/4in
Distance between rows: 25–30cm/10–12in
Harvesting: late summer (most varieties); midsummer (overwintering varieties)

Seed
Sowing time: midwinter (under glass); spring (outdoors)
Sowing distance: sow thinly
Sowing depth: 1cm/½in
Distance between rows: 25–30cm/10–12in
Thinning distance: 8–10cm/3–4in
Harvesting: late summer

HARVESTING

Onion bulbs can be lifted at any point in their growth for immediate use in the kitchen. However, for storage they must be fully developed, and the foliage should be beginning to die back. This is usually in late summer (midsummer for Japanese onions). As the foliage begins to turn yellow, lift each bulb slightly with a fork so that the roots start to break. Two weeks later carefully lift the bulbs. Clean off any soil and place them in a sunny, dry place to finish drying. A greenhouse is ideal, but they can be dried successfully outside, as long as you move them under cover at night or if rain threatens.

LEFT A good crop of onions growing in a block in a raised bed.

SOWING OUTSIDE

THINNING

HARVESTING

Sow the seeds thinly along a drill, cover with 1cm/½in soil and firm it lightly with a rake. If sowing on a heavy clay soil, a thin layer of sharp sand trickled along the bottom of the seed drill will prevent the seed from rotting before it starts to shoot.

The seedlings should germinate in 10–15 days. When they are 5–8cm/2–3in high, thin them to 8–10cm/3–4in apart. Thinnings can be used in salads. Water if conditions are very dry and keep free from weeds.

ABOVE Onions can be harvested at any time for immediate use in the kitchen, but can only be stored once they are fully mature. In late summer, when they are ready, the leaves will begin to turn brown and fall over.

STORAGE

Tie the onions into ropes or place them in net bags or on trays. They need to be in a cool, frost-free place, such as a cellar, garage or shed. Check regularly, throwing out any that show signs of rotting.

PESTS AND DISEASES

Onions can be troubled by onion eelworms, onion thrips and onion fly. The worst of these pests is onion fly, whose maggots eat the onions, turning the leaves yellow and eventually killing them. Sets are often less susceptible than seed-grown plants. Lift and destroy any infested plants. Plants infested by eelworms, which can be identified by the distorted leaves, should also be lifted and destroyed. Do not grow alliums in the same ground for several years.

Onions are also susceptible to a number of fungal and bacterial diseases, including rust, downy mildew, white rot and neck rot. Downy mildew is a particular

problem in cool, wet seasons and causes the leaves to die back. Affected bulbs will be soft and should be thrown away. Some cultivars are susceptible to bolting – the bulbs prematurely run to seed, making them useless for storing.

BELOW The leaves of these onions are beginning to brown and have been moved to one side in order to speed up this process. This also allows maximum sunlight to reach the bulbs. Although not necessary, arranging the leaves in this way gives a satisfying beauty to a practical task and keeps the garden tidy.

Growing shallots

Like onions, shallots need an open, sunny position in the garden. The soil should be light, with a pH of 6–7, and ideally it should have been dug over and manured during the previous season. Do not plant shallots in ground that has just had organic matter dug in. In the northern hemisphere shallots are traditionally planted on Boxing Day, but this is too early in most areas, and late winter or early spring is a better time.

Use a dibber to make a small hole or simply push the individual sets into the ground so that the tip is just visible and setting them at intervals of 15–18cm/6–7in. The rows should be 30cm/12in apart.

Seed can be sown in pots in late winter or early spring. Put six or seven seeds in each pot and keep them at a temperature of 7–10°C/45–50°F to germinate. Harden off the seedlings and plant them out in mid-spring, placing the clumps about 30cm/12in apart. The multiple seeds will develop in the same way as a set, and the ripening bulbs will push each other apart as they swell. Alternatively, sow the seed in drills about 1cm/½in deep and 30cm/12in apart. Thin the seedlings to 2.5–5cm/1–2in to get a single bulb from each seed. The more space you give them, the larger they will grow.

In very dry weather it will be necessary to water the shallots when the bulbs are beginning to swell, but they will not usually need to be watered. Weed regularly because they will not be able to compete with vigorous weeds.

CULTIVATION

Sowing/planting time: late winter to early spring
Planting distance: 15–18cm/6–7in
Planting depth: just below the surface
Distance between rows: 30cm/12in
Harvesting: midsummer

Hand weed rather than using a hoe so that you do not damage or disturb the shallow roots.

Shallots can be propagated by separating a cluster of bulbs and planting each one singly.

HARVESTING

When the foliage shrivels in midsummer, ease the shallots from the soil with a fork. Place them on staging in a greenhouse or on racks of wire netting to dry. Once the leaves have completely dried, remove any dirt and dead foliage and break them up into individual bulbs before leaving to dry further.

STORAGE

Place shallots on wire racks or trays or in netting bags. Store them in a dark, cool but frost-free place, such as a cellar or garage. They should keep through the winter. Check on them regularly and throw out any that show signs of rotting.

PESTS AND DISEASES

On the whole, shallots are relatively trouble free, but they may succumb to the same problems in

PLANTING SETS

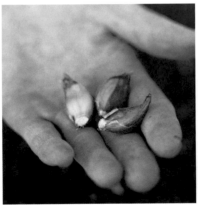

1 Shallots are generally grown from sets, although a few cultivars can be grown from seed. They grow as clumps of bulbs, each one of which may be grown on as a set. They are grown in exactly the same way as onion sets but they grow much more quickly.

2 In late winter to early spring, plant shallot bulbs in rows at 15–18cm/ 6–7in intervals with 30cm/12in between each row. The soil should be well manured the autumn before planting. Using a dibber or trowel, bury the bulbs so that only the tips are showing.

terms of pests and diseases as onions. The main pest is likely to be onion eelworm, which produces distorted leaves. Onion fly may also be a problem. They lay their eggs in the bulbs, and the maggots then go on to eat the shallots, turning the leaves yellow and eventually killing them. In both cases you will have to burn or throw away any infected bulbs. Companion planting with parsley is a traditional deterrent against the flies.

Various fungal diseases, such as neck rot and white rot, can affect shallots. Dispose of all infected bulbs to prevent further outbreaks.

RIGHT Shallots drying on netting in the sunshine before being stored tied in bunches, hung in net bags or placed in shallow trays.

BELOW Shallots growing in rows. It is possible to grow shallots either in rows or in blocks.

Growing garlic

A sunny open position is required and, as with other members of the onion family, a light soil with a pH of 6–7.5 is preferred. Use soil that has been manured for a previous crop or, if you are planting in spring, dig in the manure in the preceding autumn.

If possible plant in mid- to late autumn. In colder districts, however, and in heavy cold soils it is better to wait until spring. Remove the outer skin and break the bulbs into individual cloves. Use a dibber to plant the cloves at 10–15cm/4–6in intervals, burying them so that they are covered to about their own height with soil. Alternatively, draw out a drill about 5cm/2in deep and plant the cloves in this at 10–15cm/4–6in intervals. Allow about 30cm/12in between each row. Keep the plants well weeded, but avoid damaging the bulbs with the hoe.

Water the plants if the weather is dry for a prolonged period of time. If the variety of garlic that you are growing is hard-stemmed, it is likely that a rigid flower stem will develop. This should not affect the quality of the bulb, but the size of the cloves can be increased if the flower is cut off before it has developed too far.

HARVESTING

Lift the bulbs when the leaves have turned yellow. Spread them out in a sunny place, preferably under cover – on greenhouse staging is ideal. When they have dried out thoroughly, remove any dirt and any long roots. If you are braiding them or tying them in bunches, the leaves will need to be left on. If you are keeping them in net bags or trays, remove the dead foliage, leaving about 2.5cm/1in of stem.

STORAGE

There are several ways in which garlic can be stored, some very decoratively. The simplest is to tie the stems together so that the garlic can be hung in bunches. A more sophisticated method is to braid the leaves together so that a chain of garlic is formed. Although these

PLANTING

1 Use a dibber to make holes in the ground for each clove, at 10–15cm/4–6in intervals. A line of string will help you to keep the row straight.

2 Plant the cloves in the holes, covering them with their own depth of soil and firming them in. Plant the cloves slightly deeper in lighter soils.

ropes of garlic are decorative, resist the temptation to hang them in the kitchen because the warmth and moist air will soon bring them into growth. Hang them in a cool, but frost-free, shed or cellar. Alternatively, place the garlic in trays and keep them in a similar position.

PESTS AND DISEASES

Garlic is relatively pest free. It can, however, suffer from various fungal or viral diseases. If the problem is a minor attack of rust, it can be ignored. If it is anything else, you will have to remove the bulbs, and burn or destroy them.

ABOVE Garlic plants grow to 60cm/2ft high when mature. Greenish-white flowers only appear in warm climates.

BELOW A healthy crop of garlic plants. Unlike onions, the garlic bulbs form out of sight below the ground.

ABOVE Freshly harvested garlic with its papery white skin, ready to be cleaned and strung for storage.

Growing spring onions

Spring onions (scallions) need an open, sunny site. The soil should preferably be light, with a pH of 6–7, but they will grow in most soil as long as it is fertile but not recently manured. Dig in manure in autumn for spring sowing.

To give a supply over a long period, sow every three or four weeks in spring and summer. The seed should be sown thinly in drills 1cm/½in deep and 15–20cm/6–8in apart. Alternatively, plant in bands 8cm/3in wide and 15cm/6in apart and thin seedlings to 2.5cm/1in apart. The onions should be ready for eating after about eight weeks. For a crop in early spring, sow seed of a hardy cultivar in late summer and protect the seedlings with cloches. Onions that are overwintered will take about 36 weeks to reach maturity. Grow spring onions quickly or they will become tough.

Water the growing onions regularly and weed by hand so that the shallow roots are not damaged by a hoe. Start to harvest as soon as they are large enough, beginning with the biggest thinnings. Thereafter, pull up alternate plants,

CULTIVATION

Sowing time: early spring
Sowing distance: sow thinly
Sowing depth: 1cm/½in
Distance between rows:
    15–20cm/6–8in
Thinning distance: avoid thinning
    if possible
Successional sowing: three-week
    intervals
Harvesting: eight weeks after
    sowing

BELOW Spring onions (scallions) can be pencil-slim or have a slight swelling at the base, forming a small bulb.

THINNING

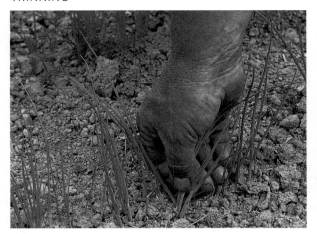

Although it is advisable to avoid thinning spring onions where possible to avoid attracting onion fly, it is often necessary to thin out congested rows.

HARVESTING

Spring onions can be harvested in lighter soils by pulling them from the ground by hand or, as shown here in heavier soils, by gently forking them out.

leaving the others to grow on. Take care when thinning because the bruised stems will attract onion fly. Some gardeners believe that growing a row of parsley next to a row of spring onions will deter onion fly.

Welsh onions are grown in the same way but should be left *in situ* because only the leaves are cropped. Lift and divide these perennials every few years when the clumps become congested with bulbs appearing above ground.

HARVESTING

Spring onions are ready for use at about eight weeks from sowing. Simply pull them from the ground. If the soil is compacted, they can be eased out with a hand fork.

STORAGE

Spring onions cannot be stored fresh for more than a few days. Keep in a cool place or in a refrigerator. The leaves can be chopped and frozen in the same way as herbs, either in bags or in ice cubes, for use as required.

PESTS AND DISEASES

The main pest is onion fly, whose maggots eat the onions, turning the leaves yellow and eventually killing them. The dangerous period is when the onions are damaged by thinning or weeding because the flies smell the odour that is given off. Burn or throw away any affected onions. Onion eelworm produces distorted leaves. Again, dispose of affected plants.

Various fungal diseases can affect spring onions, but because their life is so short any diseased plants should be destroyed and a fresh start made in a new position in the garden.

RIGHT Spring onions do not keep for long, so they are best harvested when needed, and eaten fresh.

Growing leeks

Leeks like an open, sunny position and a rich, fertile soil, with a pH of 6.5–7.5, that is reasonably free draining. Dig well-rotted manure or compost into the soil in autumn for planting in spring. Leeks like a long growing season, so start them off by sowing in nursery-bed rows in early to mid-spring. Sow thinly in drills 1cm/½in deep and 15cm/6in apart if you need more than one row. Transplant when the seedlings are 15–20cm/6–8in high, which will be two or three months after sowing. Water the row the day before lifting and then dig out in batches with a hand fork. Plant into their permanent rows using a dibber. The plants should be 15cm/6in apart and the rows should be 30cm/12in apart. Make a hole about 15cm/6in deep and drop the leek in so that about 5cm/2in of the leaves show above the soil. Do not fill in the hole with soil, but fill it with water. This will wash sufficient soil around the roots.

As the leeks grow, earth (hill) them up by pulling soil up around the stems to blanch them. Alternatively, plant the leeks in the bottom of a trench and gradually fill the trench as the leeks grow. Keep weeded and watered in the early stages of growth.

HARVESTING

Leeks can be lifted for use at any time between early autumn and late spring. Dig them out with a fork. Autumn varieties should be harvested before midwinter.

STORAGE

Leeks are generally hardy and can be left in the ground until they are required. In cold areas they can be covered over with a cloche. They are best used fresh from the ground, but they can be dug several days before use and kept in a cool place. There is no method

TRANSPLANTING

1 Make a hole with a dibber and drop the plant in. Do not fill in the hole, but leave it open.

2 Fill each hole along the row with water. Still leave the hole open; enough soil will have washed in to protect the roots.

EARTHING (HILLING) UP

Earth up the plants as they grow in order to blanch the stems. Alternatively, plant in a trench and fill it in as the plants grow.

HARVESTING

Harvest the leeks by digging under them with a fork. As you do this, pull them from the ground with the other hand.

of storing leeks out of the ground. If the piece of ground they occupy is needed for some other purpose in the spring, then they can be lifted and heeled in elsewhere until they are needed. Simply dig a trench and insert the leeks to the same depth as they were in their original planting position. Dig them up as and when they are required.

PESTS AND DISEASES

Leeks are not usually troubled by pests and diseases. Rust is the most likely problem. Infected plants can be burned or thrown away; if the rust is not too severe it can be ignored, although it is best to plant leeks elsewhere for the next year. Other onion pests and diseases may occasionally be a problem; dispose of any affected plants.

RIGHT A good block of leeks, with their rich green leaves, looks decorative in its own right.

Growing chives

Chives are hardy perennials, often grown in the herb garden or flower border rather than the vegetable garden, since their flowers are so attractive. Their round, hollow, grass-like leaves have a mild onion flavour. They like moist, fertile soil that is slightly alkaline and a position in full sun, but they will grow in almost any soil and in light shade.

Sow seed in early spring outdoors in groups of three or four in drills about 1cm/½in deep or in modules under glass. Thin to about 15cm/6in apart when the seedlings are large enough to handle.

Alternatively, buy plants in late spring. Space small groups 23cm/9in apart. Water regularly in dry weather and hand weed. After flowering, cut back the leaves to about 5cm/2in to encourage a new crop of leaves.

Divide established clumps in spring or autumn and replant in new or rejuvenated soil.

Seed can be sown in late summer to early autumn and kept indoors or under glass for a winter crop. Alternatively, dig up an established plant, cut off the leaves, plant in a pot and bring indoors.

HARVESTING

Do not cut off the leaves of spring-sown plants until late summer. Leaves can be snipped from

BELOW Use only the leaves and flowers of chives because the flower stalks are usually too tough for culinary use.

DIVIDING A CLUMP OF CHIVES

1 Although most herbaceous herbs are best divided in winter, chives can be split during the growing season. Dig up a clump of healthy chives, having first prepared a new piece of ground.

2 Use scissors or a sharp knife to cut the tops down to a few centimetres (an inch or two) to make them easier to handle and because the leaves would otherwise quickly wilt.

3 It is now easy to pull the clump apart just using your hands. If the roots are very congested, use a hand fork to force the clump into sections. Alternatively, cut into sections with a sharp knife.

4 All these smaller clumps, each with about ten stems, have been produced from a single good-sized clump of chives.

5 Replant the new clumps of chives in fertile soil with a gap of 23cm/9in between plants. Water well and they will quickly regrow.

6 Lift and divide chives every two years or so according to growth. Pot up in good-quality compost (soil mix) in autumn for forcing winter supplies indoors.

established plants. The flowers are edible, and make an attractive garnish, but the flower stems are tough and should be discarded.

STORAGE
Chives are best used fresh, but the leaves can be frozen whole or chopped and frozen in ice cubes. They can also be dried.

PESTS AND DISEASES
Chives are susceptible to the same pests and diseases as other alliums. Onion fly maggots, thrips, downy mildew and white rot can be troublesome. Rust can also be a problem: infected plants should be dug up and disposed of and new plants started elsewhere in the garden in the following season. Although not a disease, chives do suffer from overcrowding and even a single bulb will rapidly grow into a large clump, which should be regularly divided to keep them healthy.

RIGHT A white-flowered chive that is usually grown for decorative purposes, although they can be used in the kitchen as they taste the same as purple-flowered varieties.

Growing Florence fennel

Florence fennel is not easy to grow. It is an annual, which does best in rich, well-drained soil, with a pH of 5.5–7.5, which must remain moist throughout the growing period. It should also be sheltered from strong prevailing winds. Ideally, grow Florence fennel in ground that was manured during the previous season.

To minimize root disturbance, sow two or three seeds in modules under glass, or sow *in situ*. Sowing in early to midsummer is the best way to reduce the chance of bolting, but bolt-resistant cultivars may succeed if sown from mid-spring. If sowing in modules, remove all but the most strongly growing seedling and harden off before planting out at distances of 30–45cm/12–18in in all directions.

If sowing *in situ*, station-sow groups of three, 30–45cm/12–18in apart, at a depth of 1cm/½in. Thin to one per station. You can also make a sowing in late summer and bring the plants under cover for a supply of leaves in early winter, but they are unlikely to form bulbs. Encourage plants to grow quickly by watering and weeding regularly.

Most forms of this plant are sensitive to day length, and they often bolt before the bulb forms if seed is sown too early or if the summer is cold. Premature bolting also occurs if plants are subject to lack of water or to fluctuations in temperature at any point in the growing season. However, in sheltered gardens and given the right conditions this is a fast-growing plant, developing an

edible bulb within 10–15 weeks after sowing.

As the bulbs develop, earth (hill) up soil around them to keep them white and to help them taste sweeter. Water is crucial so keep the fennel plants well watered during dry spells. A mulch will help to conserve moisture.

HARVESTING

Florence fennel is ready to harvest when the bulb is about the size of a tennis ball, which is about two or three weeks after earthing up. It can either be pulled from the ground and then the root and leaf stems cut off, or cut from the root while still in the ground. This has the advantage that the root will sprout again and produce new feathery foliage that can be used for flavouring or decoration. If seed is required, the plants will have to be left in the ground for a second year, during which they will flower and set seed. This can be collected

LEFT Though a challenging vegetable to grow, Florence fennel is well worth persevering with. It produces plump bulbs that have a unique flavour, as well as being highly decorative with their finely cut, bright green leaves.

on a dry day and dried thoroughly in a warm place before being stored in an airtight jar.

STORAGE

Florence fennel is best eaten when it is fresh, straight from the garden. It will keep for a few days if it is stored in a refrigerator but not for any longer.

PESTS AND DISEASES

Florence fennel is blessed as being one of the vegetables that rarely suffers from any problems with pests and diseases. Most of the difficulties are caused by unsuitable weather or soil conditions.

HARVESTING

These Florence fennel bulbs are ready for harvesting. They can be pulled directly from the ground or cut just below the bulb so that the root produces more foliage, which can be used as a garnish.

Harvesting and storing

The harvesting of bulb vegetables depends on the length of time that they can be stored. Onions, shallots and garlic, which, if stored correctly, can keep throughout the winter, should be harvested when they are fully grown. Leeks, spring onions and chives, which have a shorter shelf life, are better left in the ground until they are needed.

ONIONS, SHALLOTS AND GARLIC

It is obvious when onions, shallots and garlic are ready to be harvested. With onions and shallots, the leaf stem keels over at the top (neck) of the bulb. With garlic, the leaves start to die back, wither and keel over. When this happens, it is fairly certain that the bulb has finished its growth for the season and is as big as it is going to get.

Sometimes onions develop a "fat" or "thick" neck. This is not a disease, but a physiological

ABOVE Once harvested, shallots are best strung for storage and kept in a dry, frost-free place. They should keep throughout the winter if stored in this way.

ABOVE Onions can be stored in trays in a frost-free shed.

condition. Some cultivars are more susceptible than others, and wet weather is an additional factor. The neck of the onion becomes thick and remains green, and the leaves do not keel over but stay upright and healthy. The onion still continues to grow, rather than to ripen and dry off. If left in the soil, the onion would eventually bolt, or run to flower. Such onions are perfectly good to eat, but they will not keep for a great length of time, so use them as quickly as possible.

When the onion leaves keel over, it is best to leave them in the soil for a week or so, especially if the weather is dry and sunny. After that, gently pull the onions up to expose the roots to the air and leave them on the ground to finish drying and for the root to wither. If the weather is cold and wet, remove the bulbs to a dry but well-ventilated place: placing them on the greenhouse staging is ideal, or on a frame made of netting. Do not remove the stems at this time. When the onions have thoroughly

dried, the stems may be twisted off and the onions placed in trays with ventilation holes.

STRINGING STEMS

If the stems are left intact, the onions may be strung together to form ropes or skeins, either by braiding the stalks together or tying them together with string or raffia. Shallots and garlic should be treated in the same way. An alternative method of "stringing" garlic is simply to thread a stiff wire through the dry necks of the bulbs.

Strung onions, shallots and garlic may then be hung up for storage, which is an excellent way of keeping them well aired. All three should keep through to the following spring if they are stored in a dry, well-ventilated room or shed that is cool and just frost-free. Check your store of onions throughout winter and discard any that feel soft. Towards the end of winter, some onions may

ABOVE A simple way of "stringing" garlic is to thread a stiff wire through the dry necks of the bulbs. The bulbs can also be tied on string.

begin to sprout. Use these immediately. Do not try to store garlic ropes in the kitchen, however decorative, or they will sprout.

SPRING ONIONS

If the spring onions have been sown thinly enough then, as they mature, you can simply pull them from the ground as and when you need them. Once pulled, they should be stored in the refrigerator, wrapped in a plastic bag.

LEEKS

These are best left in the ground rather than lifting them as they mature. Simply harvest as and when you need them in the kitchen. They will withstand quite hard frosts and can be left in the ground through autumn and into winter, until the ground is too hard to dig them up. When dug, the leeks will keep for about a week in a dry, well-ventilated room. Washed and prepared, leeks should be stored in a plastic bag in the vegetable drawer of the refrigerator.

CHIVES

These should not be pulled, but can be snipped near to the soil with a pair of kitchen scissors. Harvest chives as they are required

ABOVE A string of garlic will keep for several months if hung in a cool, dry place, such as a shed or cellar.

in the kitchen. They will keep for a few days in the refrigerator, well wrapped in a plastic bag or in an airtight container.

FLORENCE FENNEL

Florence fennel will only keep for a few days if it is stored in a refrigerator. It is best eaten straight from the garden.

HOW TO STRING ONIONS, SHALLOTS AND GARLIC

1 Take the first bulb and tie a loop of string or raffia around the neck. Pull the string tight because the necks will shrink as they dry.

2 Add more bulbs, each one just above the last, forming a loop of string around the neck of each. Bind any surplus stem into the skein.

3 When you have reached the end of the skein – usually about 12–15 onions – tie all the stalks together firmly, folding over any surplus.

Index

The publisher would like to thank the following for supplying pictures: *Tim Ellerby* 43tl; *Garden World Images* 54, 55b.